United States Presidents

Bill Clinton

Paul Joseph
ABDO Publishing Company

visit us at
www.abdopub.com

Published by ABDO Publishing Company, 4940 Viking Drive, Edina, Minnesota 55435.
Copyright © 2001 by Abdo Consulting Group, Inc. International copyrights reserved in all countries. No part of this book may be reproduced in any form without written permission from the publisher.

Printed in the United States.
Cover Photo: Corbis
Interior Photos: AP/Wide World, Archive Photos, Corbis

Contributing Editors: Bob Italia and Kate A. Furlong
Book Design and Graphics: Patrick Laurel

Library of Congress Cataloging-in-Publication Data

Joseph, Paul, 1970-
    Bill Clinton / Paul Joseph.
      p. cm. -- (United States presidents (Edina, Minn.))
    Includes index.
    ISBN 1-56239-748-6
    1. Clinton, Bill, 1946-   --Juvenile literature. 2. Presidents-
-United States--Biography--Juvenile literature. I. Title.
II. Series.
E886.J67 1998
973.929'092--dc21
   [B]   97-48572
                                        CIP
                                        AC

Contents

Bill Clinton

William Jefferson Clinton was the forty-second president of the United States. He is a talented politician. His excellent speaking skills and charm have won over many voters.

Clinton has always been interested in politics. As a student, he joined government clubs. During college, he was class president. And he worked on several political **campaigns**.

After college, Clinton taught law school. Then he decided to run for public office. He was elected **attorney general** of Arkansas. He served as governor of Arkansas for five terms.

Clinton became president in 1992 and was re-elected four years later. He worked hard to improve the **economy**. And he helped make peace in other nations. But Clinton also faced **scandals**. They led to his **impeachment**. Clinton was only the second president in U.S. history to be impeached.

The impeachment and the scandals made Clinton look bad. And they angered Americans. But Clinton kept working hard. His laws and policies helped keep America strong.

President Bill Clinton

William J. Clinton (1946-)
Forty-second President

BORN: August 19, 1946

PLACE OF BIRTH: Hope, Arkansas

ANCESTRY: English, French

FATHER: William Jefferson Blythe III (1918-1946)

STEPFATHER: Roger Clinton (1913-1967)

MOTHER: Virginia Cassidy (1923-1994)

WIFE: Hillary Rodham (1947-)

CHILDREN: Chelsea

EDUCATION: Georgetown University; Rhodes scholar at
                      Oxford University, England; Yale University

RELIGION: Baptist

OCCUPATION: Lawyer

MILITARY SERVICE: None

POLITICAL PARTY: Democratic

OFFICES HELD: Attorney General of Arkansas; Governor of Arkansas

AGE AT INAUGURATION: 46

YEARS SERVED: 1993-2001

VICE PRESIDENT: Al Gore

Birthplace of Bill Clinton

Young Billy

William Jefferson Clinton was born on August 19, 1946, in Hope, Arkansas. He was named William Jefferson Blythe IV after his father. He was called Billy when he was young.

Three months before Billy was born, his father died in a car accident. Billy's young mother, Virginia, had to raise him all by herself.

Virginia was a nurse. But she wanted to earn more money. So she moved to New Orleans, Louisiana, to get more medical training. She left Billy with her parents in Hope.

Virginia's parents were Eldridge and Edith Cassidy. They ran a grocery store in Hope. Billy's grandparents taught him to count and read.

Virginia returned to Hope when Billy was four. Then she married Roger Clinton. He ran a car dealership. In 1952, the family moved to Hot Springs, Arkansas. Soon, the Clintons had a son named Roger.

In school, Billy liked to be the center of attention. He soon became a class leader. He had many friends. Billy also was active in his church. Some people even thought he might become a minister.

At home, Billy's life was hard. His stepfather was an **alcoholic**. He **abused** Billy and Virginia. So in May 1962, Virginia divorced Roger. But that August, they got remarried. This time, Roger stopped abusing Billy and Virginia.

Billy disliked Roger. But he changed his last name from Blythe to Clinton. Billy wanted to share the same last name with his little brother.

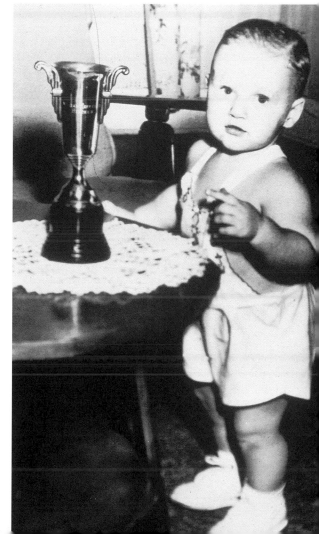

Little Billy Blythe IV

A Future Leader

*A*t Hot Springs High School, Bill was a busy student. But his mother did not let him play sports. So Bill joined other activities, such as band and student government.

Bill was a good musician. He played the saxophone. Bill competed in band contests and won many medals. Every summer, he went to band camp in Fayetteville, Arkansas.

Bill also belonged to the American Legion Boys Nation. It is a club for students interested in government. Bill went to Washington, D.C., with the Boys Nation in 1963. He visited the White House. While there, he shook hands with President Kennedy. Kennedy was Bill's hero.

In 1964, Bill graduated from high school. Then he went to Georgetown University in Washington, D.C. At Georgetown, Bill was elected class president two years in a row. He also worked as an **intern** for Arkansas **senator** William Fulbright.

Bill graduated from Georgetown in 1968. That fall, he attended Oxford University in England as a **Rhodes scholar**.

Bill studied at Oxford for two years. But he never received his **degree**. Instead, he traveled through Europe and then returned to the U.S.

Bill Clinton shakes hands with President John F. Kennedy in 1963.

The Campaign Trail

*I*n 1970, Clinton went to Yale Law School in New Haven, Connecticut. And he worked on a local politician's **campaign** for the U.S. **Senate**. He also had several jobs.

At Yale, Bill met Hillary Rodham. She was a law student, too. They spent part of 1972 working for **Democratic** senator George McGovern. He was running for president. Though McGovern lost, Bill and Hillary learned much about campaigning.

Clinton graduated from law school in 1973. He moved to Fayetteville, Arkansas. He took a job teaching at the University of Arkansas Law School. Hillary took a job in Washington, D.C.

In 1974, Clinton ran for the U.S. **Congress**. That same year, Hillary moved to Arkansas. She helped Clinton campaign. They worked hard, but he lost the race.

On October 11, 1975, Bill Clinton and Hillary Rodham got married. Clinton kept teaching law. He also stayed interested in politics. In 1976, Clinton ran for the office of Arkansas **attorney general**. He won the election. So he and Hillary moved to the state capital, Little Rock.

Clinton worked as **attorney general** for two years. But he wanted to be in a higher office. So in 1978, he ran for governor of Arkansas for the **Democratic** party. He won the election.

Bill Clinton joins George McGovern on the campaign trail in 1972.

Governor Clinton

*G*overnor Clinton had ideas for many new programs. He worked to improve schools, fix **welfare**, repair roads, and create jobs. All these programs cost money. He had to raise taxes to pay for them. This angered voters.

Clinton had other problems, too. He upset logging companies. He blamed them for cutting down too many Arkansas forests. He also angered voters when he let many Cuban **refugees** stay in Arkansas. It cost taxpayers much money.

In 1980, Bill and Hillary had a daughter. They named her Chelsea. That same year, Clinton was up for re-election. Voters were still upset about his policies. So he lost the election.

Two years later, Clinton ran for Arkansas governor again. He said he had learned from his mistakes. The voters believed him and elected him into office. Clinton went on to win the next three elections, too.

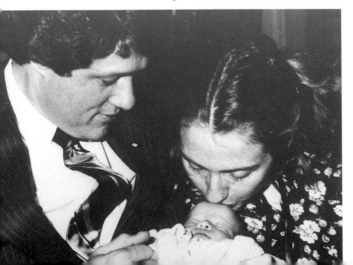

The Clinton family shortly after Chelsea's birth

Governor Clinton supported laws to improve schools. Soon, teachers were tested to be sure they knew their subjects well. Parents received fines if they did not attend conferences. And students who quit school lost their driver's licenses.

Governor Clinton improved the **economy**, too. He worked on laws that drew large companies to Arkansas. This created new, well-paying jobs. And a new plan made people get job training if they wanted to be on **welfare**.

Celebrating Clinton's election as governor in 1982

In 1992, Clinton ran for president. During the **campaign**, opponents attacked Clinton's character. They said he had dodged the **draft** and had **affairs**. But the attacks did not hurt Clinton. He won the **Democratic nomination**.

Clinton ran against President George Bush. Voters were upset with Bush because of the poor economy. So they elected Clinton as the forty-second president.

The Making of the Forty-second United States President

1946 → **1950** → **1952** → **1962** →

1946
Born August 19 in Hope, Arkansas

1950
Mother marries Roger Clinton

1952
Family moves to Hot Springs, Arkansas

1962
Mother and stepfather divorce in May and remarry each other in August; Bill changes his last name to Clinton

1970 → **1972** → **1973** → **1974** →

1970
Attends Yale Law School; meets Hillary Rodham

1972
Works on McGovern presidential campaign

1973
Graduates from Yale Law School; returns to Arkansas as a law professor

1974
Runs for U.S. Congress and loses

1980 → **1982** →

1980
Daughter Chelsea is born; Clinton loses re-election as governor

1982
Elected governor of Arkansas; re-elected as governor in the next three elections

1992
Elected president of the United States

1994
Whitewater investigation

PRESIDENTIAL

Bill Clinton

"At the dawn of the twenty-first century, a free people must now choose to shape the forces of the Information Age and the global society, to unleash the limitless potential of all our people, and yes, to form a more perfect union."

1963
Travels to Washington, D.C., and meets President Kennedy

1964
Graduates from high school; attends Georgetown University

1968
Graduates from Georgetown University; attends Oxford as a Rhodes scholar

Historic Events during Clinton's Presidency

Mars Surveyor Orbiter and Lander launched

Scottish scientists clone a sheep

Israeli president Yitzhak Rabin assassinated

1975
Marries Hillary Rodham on October 11

1976
Elected attorney general of Arkansas

1978
Elected governor of Arkansas

1996
Re-elected to a second term

1998
Impeached by the U.S. House of Representatives

1999
Found not guilty by the U.S. Senate at the impeachment trial

2000
Whitewater investigation ends; no charges filed

YEARS

President Clinton

*W*illiam Jefferson Clinton took office on January 20, 1993. Clinton quickly set up his **cabinet**. Many presidents had only white men in their cabinets. Clinton's cabinet was different. It included women, African Americans, and Hispanics.

In October 1993, Clinton sent a plan to **Congress**. It suggested ways to improve America's health care system. The plan allowed all Americans to get **insurance**. It also lowered insurance costs. Congress voted against Clinton's plan. They thought it would not work.

The Clintons faced personal problems in 1994. Some people believed they had made illegal land deals in Arkansas with the Whitewater Development Corp. The U.S. government hired Kenneth Starr to investigate the case. Clinton had to **testify** before Congress. His business partners went to jail. But the Clintons were not punished. This **scandal** is called the Whitewater **affair**.

Despite the scandal, Clinton worked hard. Congress passed many laws he supported. These laws controlled guns, raised wages, and cut government spending. Another law gave citizens time off from work to care for a new baby or a sick family member.

Clinton also worked on the North American Free Trade Agreement (NAFTA). It slowly ended **tariffs** on goods traded between the U.S., Mexico, and Canada. This improved trade. NAFTA began on January 1, 1994.

Bill Clinton takes the oath of office on January 20, 1993.

Clinton worked with other countries, too. He helped leaders from Israel and Jordan sign a peace agreement in July 1994. Later that year, he sent U.S. troops to Haiti. They returned Haiti's president to power after he had been overthrown. In 1995, Clinton wanted to stop a war in Bosnia. So he sent U.S. troops there to bring about peace.

In 1996, President Clinton ran for re-election against Robert Dole. Times were good and voters did not want a change. Clinton easily won the election.

During Clinton's second term, America had much trouble in other countries. In 1998, **terrorists** based in Afghanistan bombed U.S. **embassies** in Africa. Clinton ordered military attacks against the terrorists.

That same year, Clinton ordered military attacks against Iraq. Iraq would not let the **United Nations (U.N.)** inspect Iraqi weapons factories. The U.N. feared these factories made **weapons of mass destruction**. Iraq had agreed to these inspections after it lost the Persian Gulf War in 1991.

In March 1999, Clinton approved of **NATO** attacks on Yugoslavia. Yugoslavia had been attacking people in Kosovo. In June 1999, Yugoslav leaders agreed to stop the fighting. So NATO stopped its attack. But it sent troops to Kosovo, including 7,000 Americans. These troops kept the peace.

Soon, Clinton worked on America's trade with other countries. In 2000, Clinton supported a new law to improve trade with China. That same year, he signed a new trade agreement with Vietnam.

Back home, Clinton continued to choose women and **minorities** for important government jobs. In 1996, he named Madeleine Albright **secretary of state**. She was the first woman to head the Department of State. Clinton also named Bill Richardson as America's head **delegate** to the **U.N.** Richardson was America's first Hispanic to hold this job.

Bill Richardson and Madeleine Albright talk during a U.N. meeting.

The Seven "Hats" of the U.S. President

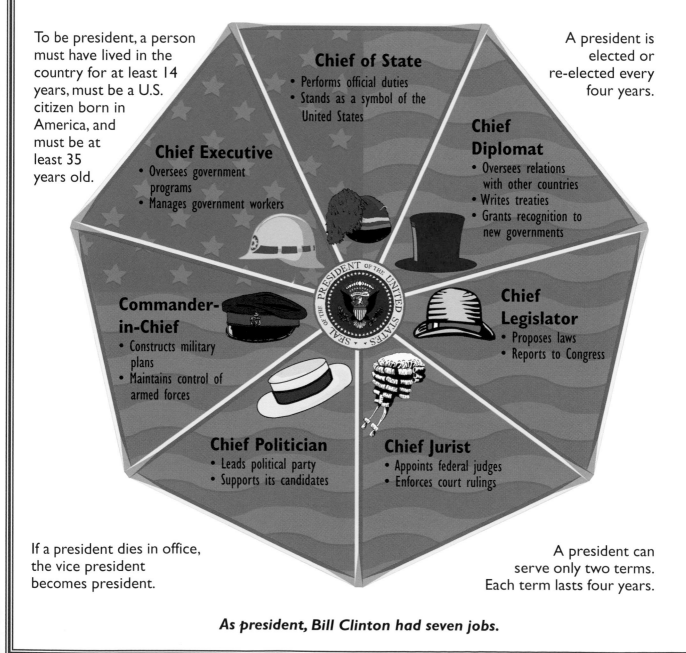

To be president, a person must have lived in the country for at least 14 years, must be a U.S. citizen born in America, and must be at least 35 years old.

A president is elected or re-elected every four years.

Chief of State
- Performs official duties
- Stands as a symbol of the United States

Chief Diplomat
- Oversees relations with other countries
- Writes treaties
- Grants recognition to new governments

Chief Executive
- Oversees government programs
- Manages government workers

Commander-in-Chief
- Constructs military plans
- Maintains control of armed forces

Chief Legislator
- Proposes laws
- Reports to Congress

Chief Politician
- Leads political party
- Supports its candidates

Chief Jurist
- Appoints federal judges
- Enforces court rulings

If a president dies in office, the vice president becomes president.

A president can serve only two terms. Each term lasts four years.

As president, Bill Clinton had seven jobs.

The Three Branches of the U.S. Government

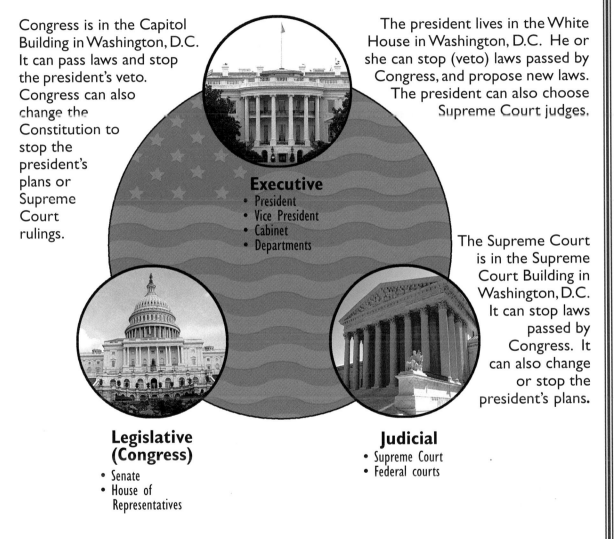

Congress is in the Capitol Building in Washington, D.C. It can pass laws and stop the president's veto. Congress can also change the Constitution to stop the president's plans or Supreme Court rulings.

The president lives in the White House in Washington, D.C. He or she can stop (veto) laws passed by Congress, and propose new laws. The president can also choose Supreme Court judges.

Executive
- President
- Vice President
- Cabinet
- Departments

The Supreme Court is in the Supreme Court Building in Washington, D.C. It can stop laws passed by Congress. It can also change or stop the president's plans.

Legislative (Congress)
- Senate
- House of Representatives

Judicial
- Supreme Court
- Federal courts

The U.S. Constitution formed three government branches. Each branch has power over the others. So no single group or person can control the country. The Constitution calls this "separation of powers."

Impeachment

*C*linton had personal problems in his second presidential term. In 1998, he had to **testify** in a **sexual harassment** lawsuit filed by Paula Jones. He swore to tell the truth.

Lawyers asked Clinton a question about Monica Lewinsky. She was a White House **intern**. They wanted to know if Clinton had an **affair** with her. He said no. Lewinsky also swore she did not have an affair with Clinton.

A judge threw out the Jones case in April 1998. But Kenneth Starr continued to investigate Clinton. Starr thought the president lied about Lewinsky in the Jones case. He thought Clinton may have asked Lewinsky to lie, too. But they both denied the charges.

On August 17, 1998, Clinton went before a **grand jury**. He swore to tell the truth. He said he and Lewinsky did not have an affair. He also said that he never asked Lewinsky to lie.

After testifying before the grand jury, Clinton went on television. He admitted he had had an "inappropriate relationship" with Lewinsky. But he still denied asking anyone to cover up the affair.

Paula Jones

Kenneth Starr

Monica Lewinsky

President Clinton swears to tell the truth before the grand jury.

In September 1998, Starr sent his final report to the **House of Representatives**. The report said Clinton may have lied in the Jones case. It said he may have lied to the **grand jury**, too. This is a crime called perjury.

Clinton settled the Jones lawsuit in November 1998. But his problems were not over. That December, the House of Representatives **impeached** Clinton. They believed he had committed perjury. They also thought he had **obstructed** justice by asking Lewinsky to lie.

Next, the **Senate** held a trial. They tried to figure out if Clinton was guilty. They also tried to figure out if Clinton should lose his job as president. In February 1999, the Senate found Clinton not guilty. He remained president.

Clinton continued to work hard in 2000. Vice President Al Gore ran for president. Clinton **campaigned** for him. Hillary ran for the U.S. Senate. Clinton campaigned for her, too.

During Bill Clinton's eight years as president, he accomplished much. He led America through a prosperous time. He helped solve problems with other countries. But he also made poor decisions in his business and personal life. These poor decisions hurt his name, and almost cost him the presidency.

THE PATH TO IMPEACHMENT

The impeachment of a government official is made possible by the Constitution of the United States. Its Articles of Impeachment state: "The President, Vice President, and all civil officers of the United States, shall be removed from office on impeachment for, and conviction of, treason, bribery, or other high crimes and misdemeanors."

The Constitution grants the House of Representatives the "sole power of impeachment." The Constitution grants the Senate the "sole power to try all impeachments."

HOUSE OF REPRESENTATIVES

1 Charges against a government official are delivered to the Speaker of the House.

2 The House creates rules to start the investigation.

3 A special House group holds a hearing. The group is called the Judiciary Committee. It suggests the Articles of Impeachment to the House.

4 The House votes on each of the Articles.

A majority vote is needed to approve impeachment. If one or more Articles are approved, the impeachment goes to the Senate for trial (see step 5). If none are approved, the impeachment process ends.

SENATE

5 The Senate hears the approved Articles of Impeachment. The vice president oversees the hearing. If the president is on trial, the Chief Justice of the Supreme Court oversees it.

6 The Senate votes on each Article of Impeachment.

If two-thirds of the Senate votes guilty on any of the Articles, the official is removed from office. If not, the official is found not guilty.

THE HISTORY OF IMPEACHMENT

Since 1797, the House of Representatives has impeached 16 government officials. Included are two presidents, a cabinet member, a senator, a Supreme Court justice, and eleven federal judges. The Senate has convicted and removed seven government officials. All were judges.

Many officials have quit before they could be impeached. The most famous of these officials is President Richard M. Nixon. He quit in 1974 because of the Watergate scandal.

Fast Facts

- When Clinton was in school, his favorite books were *The Silver Chalice*, *The Robe*, *Black Beauty*, and *The Last of the Mohicans*.

- During the 1992 presidential **campaign**, Clinton played his saxophone on the *Arsenio Hall Show*.

- Clinton was the first president to do an interview on MTV.

- The Clinton family has two pets. They have a cat named Socks and a dog named Buddy.

- President Clinton's favorite foods are chicken enchiladas, bananas, apples, and vegetable beef soup.

- President Clinton knows exercise is important. He jogs about three miles (5 km) a day and plays golf often.

Clinton plays his saxophone on the Arsenio Hall Show *in 1992.*

Glossary

abuse - to mistreat or hurt someone.

affair - a romantic relationship between two people who are not married to each other. An affair can also be an event.

alcoholic - a person who has a disease in which he or she cannot control the urge to drink alcohol.

attorney general - the chief law officer of a national or state government.

cabinet - a group of advisers chosen by the president.

campaign - an organized series of events with the goal of electing a person to public office.

Congress - the lawmaking body of the U.S. It is made up of the Senate and the House of Representatives. It meets in Washington, D.C.

degree - a title given by a college to its graduates after they have completed their studies.

delegate - a person chosen to represent others.

Democrat - a person who is liberal and believes in a large government.

draft - to be selected for military service. People who are drafted must serve in the armed forces.

economy - the way a state or nation uses its money, goods, and natural resources.

embassy - the home and office of an ambassador in a foreign country.

grand jury - a group of people that investigates a crime. It decides if there is enough evidence for a trial.

House of Representatives - the lower house in the U.S. Congress. Citizens elect members of the house to make laws for the nation.

impeach - to have a trial to decide if an elected official should be removed from office.

insurance - a contract that helps people pay their bills if they are sick or hurt. People with insurance pay money each month to keep the contract.

intern - a student who gets advanced training by working in his or her field.

minority - a racial, religious, or political group that is different from the larger group of which it is a part.

NATO - North Atlantic Treaty Organization. A group formed by the U.S., Canada, and some European countries in 1949. It tries to create peace among its nations and protect them from common enemies.

nominate - to name a person as a candidate for office.

obstruct - the act of blocking something.

refugee - a person who flees to another country for safety and protection.

Rhodes scholar - a scholarship to Oxford University. It is given to students with good grades who have shown leadership.

scandal - something that shocks people and disgraces those connected with it.

secretary of state - a member of the president's cabinet who handles problems with other countries.

Senate - the upper house in the U.S. Congress. Citizens elect senators to make laws for the nation.

sexual harassment - unwanted verbal or physical conduct related to a person's gender.

tariff - the taxes a government puts on foreign goods.

terrorist - a person who uses violence to threaten people or governments.

testify - to give evidence in a court of law while under oath.

United Nations (U.N.) - a group of nations formed in 1945. Its goals are peace, human rights, security, and social and economic development.

weapons of mass destruction - weapons that have the power to kill many people at one time.

welfare - money that the government gives to people in need.

Internet Sites

The Presidents of the United States of America
http://www.whitehouse.gov/WH/glimpse/presidents/html/presidents.html
Part of the White House Web site.

A Place Called Hope
http://www.hopeusa.com/clinton/believe.html
A site sponsored by Clinton's hometown.

These sites are subject to change. Go to your favorite search engine and type in United States Presidents for more sites.

Index